chicken

for all seasons

TRIDENT
PRESS
INTERNATIONAL

acknowledgements

Published by:
TRIDENT PRESS INTERNATIONAL
801. 12th Avenue South
Suite 400
Naples, FL 34102 U.S.A.
Copyright(c) Trident Press
Tel: (239) 649 7077
Fax: (239) 649 5832
Email: tridentpress@worldnet.att.net
Website: www.trident-international.com

Chicken for all Seasons
Compiled by: R&R Publications Marketing Pty. Ltd.
Creative Director: Paul Sims
Production Manager: Anthony Carroll
Food Photography: Warren Webb
Food Stylists: Stephane Souvlis, Janet Lodge, Di Kirby
Recipe Development: Ellen Argyriou, Sheryle Eastwood, Kim Freedman,
Lucy Kelly, Donna Hay
Proof Reader: Andrea Hazell-Tarttelin

Includes Index
ISBN 1 58279466 9
EAN 9 781582 79466 2
UPC 6 15269 94669 5

Second Edition 2003
Computer Typeset in Humanist 521
& Times New Roman

Printed in Colombia

Contents

introduction

The chicken has always been a valuable food source. From the earliest recorded history, it has appeared on the tables of ancient Egypt, Greece, Rome and Asia.

The ancestor of the chicken of today is thought to be the Indian Jungle Fowl which was domesticated by the Indus Valley civilisation in about 2500 BC. It is not known how the bird travelled to other areas, but travel it did. The chicken has been used by almost all cultures throughout the world in their cooking pots, with each adding aspects of their culinary heritage to this versatile meat. With our rich diversity of cultures our repertoire of chicken dishes has expanded to new dimensions, and continues to expand. Ethnic dishes from other countries, such as Tandoori Chicken, Chicken Cacciatore and Hawaiian Chicken are just as popular in the world as the traditional roast chicken.

Through the pages of this book you will experience the new flavour combinations which have resulted from our culinary cultural exchange, presented in simple and quick-to-prepare recipes.

Chicken production today has made available not only the bird dressed and ready for the pot, but also each cut portioned out so you can buy as needed. Gone are the days when the favourite part of the family chicken, usually the breast, was the most popular piece.

Nutritional Value

Chicken is high in first class protein, which means it has all of the essential amino acids. Vitamins, particularly A and the B group vitamins, are well represented, as are minerals including Iron and Zinc. It is a light, tender meat which makes it easy to chew and easy to digest, so it is especially suitable for infants, children and the elderly. When the skin is removed, chicken is even lower in fat, making it an ideal food for everyone.

Purchasing and Storage of Chicken

Chicken may be purchased fresh or frozen, whole or in pieces. The choice is for the individual to make, depending on how and when one wishes to prepare and eat the chicken.

Fresh Chicken:

• When purchasing fresh chicken, make it the last purchase on your shopping trip. It is advisable to take along an insulated bag to place the chicken in to keep it cold on the trip home.

- When arriving home with your chicken purchase, remove from package (if any), rinse and wipe dry with a paper towel. Cover loosely with plastic wrap and refrigerate immediately. Fresh chicken may be kept in the refrigerator for 3 days. Place in the coldest part of the refrigerator, below 4°C/39°F.

- If chicken needs to be stored longer, it is better to buy ready frozen chicken than to buy fresh and freeze at home.

- If the chicken pieces are to be purchased and frozen for future use, make sure they are fresh. Wipe dry with paper towel then pack flat in plastic freezer bags. Extract air by pushing out towards the opening, and tape bag closed. Label and date packages.

Frozen chicken

- When purchasing frozen chicken, check that the packages are not torn.

- Place in freezer immediately you return home.

- Thaw frozen chicken thoroughly before cooking to avoid toughening the texture and to reduce the chance of some parts being undercooked. Undercooked parts could harbour food-spoiling bacteria.

- Do not refreeze thawed chicken. It is advisable to cook the thawed chicken and freeze it when cooked.

- To thaw frozen chicken, remove from wrap, place on a rack in a dish to allow liquid to collect beneath the chicken. Do not touch it. Cover loosely with plastic wrap and place in the refrigerator for 24 hours.

  This is the safest way to thaw. Thawing on the kitchen bench encourages the growth of bacteria and should be avoided.

preparation

As with all perishable foods, there are simple rules to follow in the preparation and handling of chicken. Adhering to these rules will lessen the likelihood of bacterial growth, and thereby increase the quality, flavour and enjoyment of your dishes. Many of these rules also apply to other perishable foods. They should become a common part of your kitchen routine.

Food producers and retailers maintain high standards of quality assurance and cleanliness so that we can buy safe and wholesome foods with confidence.

Consumers need to ensure that they maintain these quality and safety standards after purchase. Perishable foods, including chicken, need special attention to prevent deterioration and possible food poisoning.

Purchasing and storage instructions are provided in the introduction to this book, and should be followed at all times. The safe handling tips listed below should be employed to avoid encouraging bacterial growth and transfer.

Safe Food Handling Tips:

- Wash hands thoroughly before handling fresh chicken and other foods. Wash again before handling other food.

- Chopping boards, knives and other utensils must be washed with hot soapy water after handling raw chicken and other raw foods to prevent cross-contamination .

- Always keep cold food at 4°C/39°F or below in a refrigerator.

- Never keep raw chicken at room temperature for longer than 1 hour, including preparation time.

- Poultry must be cooked through to the centre, not left rare. This ensures that all bacteria have been killed by the heat penetration. To test, insert a skewer into the centre of the chicken or portion - if the juice runs clear the chicken is cooked through.

- Stuffing should be treated with special care. Bacteria from raw poultry can grow in the stuffing. Stuff loosely, only 2/3 full, just before cooking and remove the stuffing immediately after cooking.

- Cool cooked foods quickly by placing them in the refrigerator. Large quantities of food should be divided into smaller portions to allow quicker cooking. This relates particularly to simmered chicken and chicken stock. Do not be afraid to place hot foods in the refrigerator - it is built to take them.

- Store raw and cooked foods separately, with cooked foods at the top and raw foods at the bottom on a tray or plate.

Do not let juices drop onto other foods.

- *Understand that the danger zone for bacterial growth is between 4°C/39°F and 65°C/149°F, so keep foods cold (below 4°C/39°F) or hot (above 65°C/150°F). Food must not be left to stand on the kitchen bench as room temperature is in the danger zone.*

- *When reheating cooked chicken, bring to 75°C/167°F and hold there for a few minutes.*

Tips for Cooking Chicken in the Microwave

Whole Chicken:

1. *The microwave does not brown the chicken as the conventional oven does but a brown appearance can be achieved by either rubbing the surface with paprika, or brushing it over with a glaze.*

2. *Tie legs together with string or a strip of plastic or an elastic band to give a more even cooking shape.*

3. *Calculate the cooking time simply by doubling the size number on the chicken; e.g. No, 15 is cooked for 30 minutes and cook on MEDIUM/HIGH. Larger chickens are more successful if cooked on MEDIUM/HIGH for the first half of the cooking time, then reduce the power to MEDIUM for the remainder adding 5-8 minutes cooking time per kg.*

4. *Remember the starting temperature of the chicken will affect cooking time. A refrigerated chicken will take a few minutes longer than one at room temperature. It is advisable to cook the chicken on HIGH for the first 3-5 minutes to warm the surface then reduce power to MEDIUM/HIGH for remainder of the cooking time.*

Chicken Pieces

1 *Arrange chicken pieces with the thicker part to the outside of the dish or roasting rack for even cooking.*

2 *Rearrange pieces that are in the centre to the outside halfway through cooking.*

3 *Chicken casseroles cook better if chicken is cut into small even pieces; i.e. breast cut into 2 pieces, and thigh separated from drumstick.*

4 *Chicken pieces may be browned in a browning dish before adding to a casserole, or browned in a frying pan before microwaving. You may prefer to remove skins before placing in a casserole as they do tend to become a little rubbery.*

5 *Chicken pieces may be crumbed then cooked on a roasting rack. The result is very successful. Choose a deep-coloured dried bread crumb and add dried herbs, lemon, pepper or toasted sesame seeds. The crumbs will remain crisp.*

Breast fillets

Thigh fillets

Chicken Tenderloins

Chicken Marylard

Thigh - with bone

Chicken breast on the bone - half breast

Stir-fry pieces

Chicken mince

Wings-whole

Wings-mini drums

Wings-mid drums

Thigh Cutlets (or chicken cuts)

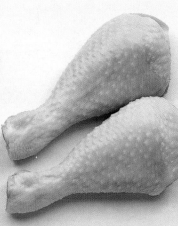

Drumsticks

Lovely legs (skinless drumsticks)

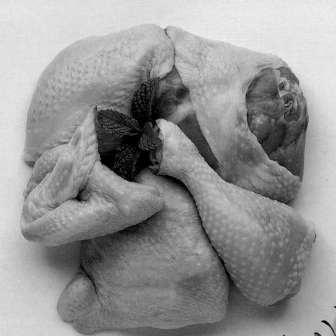

Casserole pieces

Chicken Cuts
– the way they look

The skinless cuts (breasts, breast fillets, thigh fillets and lovely legs) are extremely low in fat and are a boon to the health conscious and those watching their fat and kilojoule intake. Stir-fry pieces and chicken mince are sometimes available ready-prepared. If not, use chicken breast fillets or chicken thigh fillets and cut into strips for stir-frying or pass though a mincer or food processor for delicious, low fat chicken mince.

chicken wings moroccan style

autumn delights

With the advent of winter, autumn

gives us the opportunity to use the last of the summer ingredients. Dishes such as Chicken Roasted Capsicum. Olive and Feta Pie and a Spicy Corn and Lentil Chowder, allows the use of summer ingredients with winter cookery methods.

chicken
wings moroccan style

Photograph page 11

Method:

1 *Heat oil in a wide-based saucepan or lidded skillet, add chicken wings a few at a time and brown lightly on both sides. Remove to a plate as they brown.*

2 *Add onions and fry for 2 minutes. Stir in garlic, ginger and spices. Cook, while stirring for 1 minute, return chicken to the pan, stir and turn the wings to coat with spices.*
Add vinegar and apricot nectar, season to taste. Cover and simmer for 25 minutes.

3 *Add prunes, apricots, honey and lemon juice. Cover and simmer 10 minutes and then remove lid and simmer uncovered for 5 minutes. If a thicker sauce is desired, remove wings and fruit to a serving platter, increase heat and boil until sauce reduces and thickens, stirring occasionally.*
Pour sauce over wings. Serve immediately with steamed couscous or rice.

Serves 3-4

ingredients

2 tablespoons oil
1kg/2 lb tray chicken wings
1 large onion, finely chopped
1 clove garlic, crushed
1 1/2 teaspoons chopped fresh ginger
1/2 teaspoon ground turmeric
1/2 teaspoon cumin
1/2 cinnamon stick
1/4 cup/60ml/2fl oz cider vinegar
450g/15oz can apricot nectar
salt, pepper
100g/3oz dried prunes, pitted
100g/3oz dried apricots
1 tablespoon honey
1/4 cup/60ml/2fl oz lemon juice
steamed couscous or rice to serve

autumn delights

greek style
chicken rissoles in tomato sauce

ingredients

Rissoles
500g/1 lb chicken mince
1 medium onion (grated)
2 tablespoons parsley (finely chopped)
1/2 teaspoon salt
pepper
1 egg
1/2 cup/60g/2oz breadcrumbs (dried)
1 tablespoon water
oil (for frying)

Tomato Sauce
1 medium onion (finely chopped)
1 clove garlic (crushed)
1 tablespoon oil
1 x 440g/15oz can tomatoes
1 tablespoon tomato paste
1/2 cup/120ml/4fl oz water
1/2 teaspoon oregano (dried)
1 teaspoon sugar
salt, pepper
1 tablespoon parsley (chopped)

Method:

1 *Place chicken mince in a bowl, grate onion into the mince, and add remaining ingredients. Mix well to combine, and knead a little by hand. With wet hands roll into balls. Heat oil (1cm deep) in a frying pan, and sauté the rissoles until they change colour on both sides. Remove to a plate.*

2 *To the pan add the onion and garlic, and sauté a little. Add remaining sauce ingredients, and bring to the boil. Return the rissoles to the pan, reduce heat, and simmer (covered) for 30 minutes.*

3 *Serve over boiled spaghetti or other pasta.*

Serves 4-6

chicken

roasted capsicum, olive & feta pie

chicken roasted capsicum (pepper), olive & feta pie

ingredients

2 tablespoons olive oil
I large leek, washed and sliced
I clove garlic, crushed
500g/1 lb chicken breasts, diced
I bunch English spinach, washed and blanched
2 red capsicum (peppers), roasted and diced
60g/2oz black olives, pitted and halved
200g/7oz feta cheese, crumbled
2 tablespoons parsley, chopped
I tablespoon oregano, chopped
3 eggs
60ml/2fl oz cream
freshly ground pepper
8-16 sheets filo pastry
I tablespoon olive oil (extra)
I tablespoon butter, melted
I tablespoon sesame seeds

Method:

1 Pre-heat oven to 180°C/350°F.
2 Heat one tablespoon oil in a large fry pan, add leek and garlic, and cook for five minutes or until soft. Set aside.
3 Heat extra oil, add chicken in batches, and cook for 6-8 minutes.
4 Drain spinach, squeeze out excess water, and chop roughly.
5 In a large bowl, combine chicken, spinach, capsicum (peppers), olives, feta, parsley, oregano, eggs, cream and pepper. Stir until well combined. Set aside.
6 Lightly grease a 23 x 23cm/9 x 9in square baking dish. Combine the extra oil and butter.
7 Lay out sheets of filo, put two together, and brush with the oil mixture. Put another two on top, and brush again. Continue to repeat this until you have four double sheets. Line the baking dish with the filo, and trim around the edges. Fill with the chicken mixture. Brush the remaining sheets with oil (the same as before, using the same amount). Place the filo on top of the baking dish, tucking the edges inside the baking dish.
8 Brush the top with the oil mixture, sprinkle with sesame seeds, and bake in the oven for 40-45 minutes.

Serves 4-6

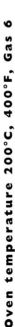
chicken
and leek roll

Method:

1 Melt butter in a frying pan over a medium heat, add leeks and cook, stirring, for 4 minutes or until leeks are golden. Add mushrooms and cook for 2 minutes longer or until mushrooms are soft. Remove from pan and set aside to cool.

2 Add chicken to pan and cook, stirring, for 5 minutes or until chicken is just cooked. Remove chicken from pan and set aside to cool.

3 Place leek mixture, chicken, sour cream, chives and black pepper to taste in a bowl and mix to combine.

4 Brush each pastry sheet with oil and layer. Spread filling over pastry leaving a 2cm/³/₄in border. Fold in sides and roll up like a Swiss roll. Place roll on a baking tray, brush with oil and sprinkle with poppy seeds. Bake for 20 minutes or until pastry is crisp and golden.

Serves 4

ingredients

30g/1oz butter
3 leeks, sliced
125g/4oz button mushrooms, sliced
2 boneless chicken breast fillets, sliced
¹/₃ cup/90g/3oz sour cream
1 tablespoon snipped fresh chives
freshly ground black pepper
12 sheets filo pastry
2 tablespoons olive oil
1 tablespoon poppy seeds

Oven temperature 200°C, 400°F, Gas 6

chicken
pasta gratin

Method:

1 Brush tomatoes with oil and cook under a preheated hot grill for 10 minutes or until soft and browned. Set aside.

2 Cook pasta in boiling water in a large saucepan following packet directions, drain and set aside.

3 Melt butter in a frying pan over a medium heat, add garlic and onion and cook, stirring, for 3 minutes or until onion is soft and golden. Add chicken and cook, stirring, for 6 minutes longer or until chicken is tender.

4 Stir wine, cream and tarragon into pan and bring to the boil. Reduce heat and simmer for 10 minutes. Remove pan from heat, add tomatoes, pasta, half the tasty cheese (mature Cheddar) and black pepper to taste and mix gently to combine.

5 Spoon mixture into a greased 8 cup/ 2 litre/3¹/₂pt capacity ovenproof dish. Combine remaining tasty cheese (mature Cheddar) and Parmesan cheese and sprinkle over pasta mixture. Bake for 20 minutes or until cheese melts and is golden.

ingredients

6 plum (egg or Italian) tomatoes, halved
1 tablespoon vegetable oil
315g/10oz wholemeal pasta shapes
30g/1oz butter
1 clove garlic, crushed
1 red onion, sliced
2 boneless chicken breast fillets, sliced
¹/₄ cup/60ml/2fl oz white wine
1¹/₄ cups/315ml/10fl oz cream (double)
1 tablespoon chopped fresh tarragon
or 1 teaspoon dried tarragon
125g/4oz grated tasty cheese
(mature Cheddar)
freshly ground black pepper
30g/1oz grated Parmesan cheese

Serves 4

chicken
moussaka

Method:

1 *Place eggplant (aubergine) slices in a colander set over a bowl and sprinkle with salt. Set aside to stand for 10 minutes then rinse under cold running water and pat dry with absorbent kitchen paper.*

2 *Heat 2 tablespoons oil in a frying pan over a medium heat and cook eggplant (aubergine) slices in batches for 2 minutes each side or until golden. Set aside.*

3 *Heat remaining oil in frying pan, add garlic and onion and cook, stirring, for 3 minutes or until onion is soft and golden. Add chicken and cook, stirring, for 5 minutes or until chicken browns. Stir in tomatoes and bring to the boil. Reduce heat and simmer for 15 minutes, or until mixture reduces and thickens. Remove pan from heat and set aside to cool.*

4 *To make sauce, melt butter in a saucepan over a medium heat, stir in flour and cook for 1 minute. Remove pan from heat and gradually stir in milk. Return pan to heat and cook, stirring constantly, until sauce boils and thickens. Remove pan from heat and stir in tasty cheese (mature Cheddar).*

5 *Arrange half the eggplant (aubergine) slices over base of a 10 cup/2¹/₂ litre/4pt capacity ovenproof dish. Top with half the chicken mixture, half the potatoes and half the cheese sauce. Repeat layers to use all ingredients. Combine breadcrumbs and Parmesan cheese and sprinkle over moussaka. Bake for 50 minutes or until top is golden and moussaka is cooked through.*

Note: *The addition of chicken to this moussaka recipe is a refreshing alternative to a traditional dish which is more often made with lamb or beef mince.*

Serves 8

ingredients

**4 large eggplant (aubergines),
thinly sliced
salt
3 tablespoons olive oil
2 cloves garlic, crushed
1 onion, chopped
500g/1 lb chicken mince
2 x 440g/14oz canned peeled
tomatoes, undrained and mashed
500g/1 lb potatoes, thinly sliced
¹/₂ cup/30g/1oz breadcrumbs, made
from stale bread
60g/2oz grated Parmesan cheese**

**Cheese sauce
30g/1oz butter
2 tablespoons flour
1¹/₄ cups/315ml/10fl oz milk
60g/2oz grated tasty cheese
(mature Cheddar)**

Oven temperature 180°C, 350°F, Gas 4

oriental
chicken pizza

Method:

1 Place pizza base on a lightly greased baking tray. Spread base with teriyaki sauce and top with chicken, snow peas (mangetout), spring onions, tofu and asparagus. Sprinkle with coriander (cilantro) and sesame seeds.

2 Drizzle chilli sauce over pizza and bake for 30 minutes or until base is golden and crisp.
Note: For a complete meal serve this tasty pizza with a selection of your favourite salads. Sweet soy sauce also known as kechap manis can be used instead of teriyaki in this recipe if you wish.

Serves 4

ingredients

I packaged 30cm/12in pizza base
¼ cup/60ml/2fl oz thick teriyaki sauce
2 boneless chicken breast fillets,
cooked and sliced
125g/4oz snow peas (mangetout),
thinly sliced
4 spring onions, sliced
155g/5oz tofu, chopped
6 asparagus spears, cut into 5cm/2in pieces
3 tablespoons chopped fresh coriander
(cilantro)
3 tablespoons sesame seeds, toasted
2 tablespoons sweet chilli sauce

Oven temperature 200°C, 400°F, Gas 6

italian
chicken in a pan

Method:

1 Place chicken between sheets of greaseproof paper and pound lightly to flatten. Dust with flour, then dip in egg and finally coat with breadcrumbs. Place on a plate lined with plastic food wrap and refrigerate for 15 minutes.

2 Heat oil in a large frying pan over a medium heat, add chicken and cook for 2-3 minutes each side or until golden. Remove from pan and set aside.

3 Add pasta sauce to pan and cook over a medium heat, stirring, for 4-5 minutes or until hot. Place chicken in a single layer on top of sauce, then top each fillet with a slice of prosciutto or ham, a slice of cheese and a sprig of sage. Cover and simmer for 5 minutes or until chicken is cooked through and cheese melts. Serve immediately.

Serves 6

ingredients

6 boneless chicken breast fillets, skinned
seasoned flour
1 egg, beaten
dried breadcrumbs
¼ cup/60ml/2fl oz vegetable oil
500g/1 lb bottled tomato pasta sauce
6 slices prosciutto or ham
6 slices mozzarella cheese
6 sprigs fresh sage

crisp
curried wings

Method:

1 Rinse the chicken wings and pat dry with kitchen paper. Rub the curry paste well onto the chicken wings with your fingers, covering all surfaces. Pin back the wing tip to form a triangle. Place in single layer on a tray; stand for 30 minutes in refrigerator, uncovered.

2 Meanwhile place the rice in a 8cup/2lt/70fl oz casserole dish; add salt and boiling water. Cover with lid or foil and place on lower shelf of oven, preheated to 180°C/350°F. Cook for 40 minutes. Remove from oven and stand covered 5 minutes.

3 Transfer chicken wings to a wire rack placed over a baking tray. Place on top shelf of oven above the rice. Cook for 20 minutes, turning once. When rice has been removed, increase oven temperature to 200°C/400°F for 5 minutes to crisp the wings.

For the Sambal: Halve the tomatoes and remove the seeds then cut into small dice.

Peel cucumber; slice in half lengthwise, remove the seeds with a teaspoon. Dice the cucumber and mix with the diced tomato. Place in a suitable dish, place chutney in a similar dish. Serve the crisp curried wings with the rice and accompanying sambals.

Tip: Co-ordinate the cooking so that rice and chicken utilise the same oven.

Serves 4-6

ingredients

1kg/2lb chicken wings
2 tablespoons mild curry paste
1½ cups/330g/110x basmati rice, rinsed
½ teaspoon salt
3 cups/750ml/24fl oz boiling water
2 tomatoes, blanched
and skinned
1 small cucumber
1 cup/240g/8oz fruit chutney

chicken and corn chowder

winter warmers

As winter sets in and the days

become shorter and the nights colder, a steaming soup, aromatic curry or a flavoursome casserole is the perfect remedy for warmth and satisfaction.

chicken
and corn chowder

Photograph page 27

Method:

1 *Heat oil in a saucepan over a medium heat, add onion and cook, stirring, for 4-5 minutes or until onion is soft. Add chicken and cook for 2 minutes longer or until chicken just changes colour.*

2 *Add potatoes and stock and bring to the boil. Reduce heat and simmer for 10 minutes or until potatoes are almost cooked. Stir sweet corn, milk, bay leaf and black pepper to taste into stock mixture and bring to the boil. Reduce heat and simmer for 3-4 minutes or until potatoes are cooked. Remove bay leaf. Stir in lemon juice, parsley, chives and black pepper to taste. Just prior to serving, sprinkle with Parmesan cheese.*

Note: *To chop the sweet corn, place in a food processor or blender and process using the pulse button until the sweet corn is coarsely chopped. Creamed sweet corn can be used in place of the kernels if you wish. If using creamed sweet corn there is no need to chop it.*

Serves 6

ingredients

1 tablespoon vegetable oil
1 small onion, diced
250g/8oz boneless chicken breast fillets, shredded
3 potatoes, chopped
3¹/₂cups/875ml/1¹/₂pt chicken stock
315g/10oz canned sweet corn kernels, drained and coarsely chopped
1¹/₄cups/315ml/10fl oz milk
1 bay leaf
freshly ground black pepper
1 tablespoon lemon juice
2 tablespoons chopped fresh parsley
1 tablespoon snipped fresh chives
60g/2oz grated Parmesan cheese

mulligatawny
soup

Method:

1 Heat oil in a large saucepan over a medium heat, add onions, apple and garlic and cook, stirring, for 5 minutes or until onions are tender. Add lemon juice, curry powder, sugar, cumin and coriander and cook over a low heat, stirring, for 10 minutes or until fragrant.

2 Blend flour with a little stock and stir into curry mixture. Add chicken, rice and remaining stock to pan and stirring constantly, bring to the boil. Reduce heat, cover and simmer for 20 minutes or until chicken and rice are cooked. Season to taste with black pepper.

Note: A dash of chilli sauce and a chopped tomato are delicious additions to this soup. Serve with crusty bread rolls, naan or pita bread.

Serves 4

ingredients

1 tablespoon vegetable oil
2 onions, chopped
1 green apple (cored, peeled and chopped)
1 clove garlic, crushed
2 tablespoons lemon juice
1 tablespoon curry powder
1 teaspoon brown sugar
$1/2$ teaspoon ground cumin
$1/4$ teaspoon ground coriander
2 tablespoons flour
8 cups/2 litres/$3^1/2$pt chicken stock
500g/1 lb boneless chicken breast or thigh fillets, cut into 1 cm/$^1/2$in cubes
$1/3$ cup/75g/$2^1/2$oz rice
freshly ground black pepper

chicken
minestrone

Method:

1 Lightly spray base of large saucepan with canola oil spray. Add onion and garlic, stirring over heat until they colour a little. Add celery and carrot and continue to stir for 1 minute.

2 Chop tomatoes and add to the saucepan with the juice. Stir in water, pepper, oregano, spice and parsley. Bring to the boil and add the macaroni. Stir until soup returns to the boil, turn down to a simmer and cook for 15 minutes.

3 Stir in cabbage, peas and chicken stirfry. Simmer for 15-20 minutes. Serve hot with crusty bread.

Tip: Left-over soup may be frozen for later use.

Serves 4-6

ingredients

canola oil spray
1 onion, finely chopped
1 clove garlic, chopped
1 stick celery, diced
1 carrot, peeled and diced
**420g/14oz can peeled tomatoes
(no added salt)**
4 cups/1 litre/35fl oz water
freshly ground black pepper
1 teaspoon dried oregano
1 teaspoon mixed spice
2 tablespoons chopped parsley
1/2 cup/60g/2oz cut macaroni
1/4 cabbage, shredded
150g/5oz frozen baby peas
200g/7oz chicken stir-fry

roasted tomato
red capsicum (pepper) and bread soup

Method:

1 Preheat the oven to 220°C/440°F.

2 Lightly oil a baking dish, place tomatoes in the dish and bake for 20 minutes or until the skins have blistered. Set aside to cool, then remove skins and roughly chop.

3 Heat the oil in a saucepan, add the garlic and the onion, and cook for 5 minutes or until soft. Add cumin and coriander, and cook for 1 minute until well combined. Add tomatoes, capsicums and stock to the saucepan, bring to the boil, and simmer for 30 minutes. Add the bread, balsamic vinegar and salt & pepper, and cook a further 5-10 minutes.

4 Serve with Parmesan cheese (if desired).

Serves 4

1kg/2 lb Roma tomatoes, roasted
2 red capsicums (peppers), roasted
and roughly chopped
30ml/10z olive oil
2 onions, finely chopped
3 cloves garlic, crushed
2 teaspoons ground cumin
1 teaspoon ground coriander
4cups/1 litre/35fl oz chicken stock
2 slices white bread, crusts removed
and torn into pieces
30ml/1 oz balsamic vinegar
salt & freshly ground pepper (to taste)

coq au vin

Method:

1 Toss chicken in flour to coat. Shake off excess flour and set aside.

2 Heat oil in a large, nonstick frying pan over a medium heat and cook chicken in batches, turning frequently, for 10 minutes or until brown on all sides. Remove chicken from pan and drain on absorbent kitchen paper.

3 Add garlic, onions or shallots and bacon to pan and cook, stirring, for 5 minutes or until onions are golden. Return chicken to pan, stir in stock and wine and bring to the boil. Reduce heat, cover and simmer, stirring occasionally, for 1 1/4 hours or until chicken in tender. Add mushrooms and black pepper to taste and cook for 10 minutes longer.

Serves 6

ingredients

2kg/4lb chicken pieces
1/2 cup/60g/2oz seasoned flour
2 tablespoons olive oil
2 cloves garlic, crushed
12 pickling onions or shallots, peeled
8 rashers bacon, chopped
1 cup/250ml/8fl oz chicken stock
3 cups/750ml/1 1/4 pt red wine
250g/8oz button mushrooms
freshly ground black pepper

cashew nut
butter chicken

Method:

1 Melt ghee or butter in a saucepan over a medium heat, add garlic and onions and cook, stirring, for 3 minutes or until onions are golden.

2 Stir in curry paste, coriander and nutmeg and cook for 2 minutes or until fragrant. Add chicken and cook, stirring, for 5 minutes or until chicken is brown.

3 Add cashews, cream and coconut milk, bring to simmering and simmer, stirring occasionally, for 40 minutes or until chicken is tender.

To roast cashews, spread nuts over a baking tray and bake at 180°C/350°F for 5-10 minutes or until lightly and evenly browned. Toss back and forth occasionally with a spoon to ensure even browning. Alternatively, place nuts under a medium grill and cook, tossing back and forth until roasted.

ingredients

60g/2oz ghee or butter
2 cloves garlic, crushed
2 onions, minced
1 tablespoon curry paste
1 tablespoon ground coriander
1/2 teaspoon ground nutmeg
750g/1 1/2 lb boneless chicken thigh or breast fillets, cut into 2cm/3/4 in cubes
60g/2oz cashews, roasted and ground
1 1/4 cups/315ml/10fl oz cream (double)
2 tablespoons coconut milk

Serves 6

moroccan
beans

Method:

1 *Heat oil in a saucepan over a medium heat, add ginger, cinnamon, cumin seeds, and turmeric and cook, stirring, for 1 minute. Add onions and cook for 3 minutes longer or until onions are soft.*

2 *Add red kidney beans, soy beans, chickpeas, chicken (if using), tomato paste (purée) and stock to pan and bring to the boil. Reduce heat and simmer for 10 minutes.*

3 *Add currants and pine nuts and cook for 2 minutes longer.*

   Note: *For a complete meal, be sure to serve this delicious mix with a hearty wholegrain bread so that all the essential amino acids are present to build complete protein.*

Serves 4-6

ingredients

1 tablespoon vegetable oil
1 tablespoon grated fresh ginger
1 teaspoon ground cinnamon
1 teaspoon cumin seeds
1/2 teaspoon turmeric
2 onions, chopped
440g/14oz canned red kidney beans,
rinsed and drained
440g/14oz canned soy beans,
rinsed and drained
440g/14oz canned chickpeas,
rinsed and drained
375g/12oz chopped cooked chicken (optional)
440g/14oz canned tomato paste (purée)
1 cup/250ml/8fl oz vegetable stock
75g/2¹/₂oz currants
60g/2oz pine nuts, toasted

smoked
chicken papperdelle

Method:

1 *To make Nasturtium Butter, place butter, garlic, lime juice and flowers in a bowl, mix well to combine and set aside.*

2 *Cook pasta in boiling water in a large saucepan following packet directions. Drain, set aside and keep warm.*

3 *Heat a nonstick frying pan over a medium heat, add chicken and cook, stirring, for 1 minute. Add wine, cream, chives and black pepper to taste, bring to simmering and simmer for 2 minutes. To serve, top pasta with chicken mixture and Nasturtium Butter.*

Note: *The perfect accompaniment to this dish is a salad of watercress or rocket tossed in balsamic vinegar and topped with shavings of Parmesan cheese. The Nasturtium butter is also delicious as a sandwich filling when teamed with watercress or rocket.*

Serves 6

ingredients

750g/1½lb pappardelle
1½kg/3lb smoked chicken, skin removed and flesh sliced
½ cup/125ml/4fl oz white wine
1 cup/250ml/8fl oz cream
2 tablespoons snipped fresh chives
freshly ground black pepper

Nasturtium Butter
125g/4oz butter, softened
1 clove garlic, crushed
1 tablespoon lime juice
6 nasturtium flowers, finely chopped

apricot
chicken

Photograph opposite

ingredients

**1¹/₂kg/ 3lb chicken pieces
1 onion, sliced
45g/1¹/₂oz packet French onion or
chicken noodle soup
2 teaspoons curry powder
440g/14oz canned apricot halves in
natural juice
¹/₄ cup/60ml/2fl oz white wine
or water**

Method:

1 Arrange chicken pieces in a large ovenproof dish. Scatter with onion, then sprinkle with soup mix and curry powder.
2 Combine apricots with juice and wine or water, pour over chicken and mix to combine. Cover and bake for 1-1¹/₄ hours or until chicken is tender.

Note: Chicken can be one of the least expensive bases for a main course, especially if you purchase the more economical chicken pieces such as legs, wings or thigh fillets.

Serves 6

Oven temperature 180°C, 350°F, Gas 4

chicken
stroganoff

Photograph opposite

ingredients

**2 tablespoons olive oil
1 onion, sliced
1 clove garlic, crushed
8 chicken thigh fillets or 4 boneless
chicken breast fillets, sliced
125g/4oz button mushrooms, sliced
1¹/₄ cups/315g/10oz sour cream
¹/₄ cup/60ml/ fl oz tomato paste
(pureé)
¹/₂ teaspoon paprika
freshly ground black pepper
2 spring onions, chopped or
chopped fresh parsley**

Method:

1 Heat oil in a frying pan over a medium heat, add onion and garlic and cook, stirring, for 4-5 minutes or until onion is tender. Add chicken and cook, stirring, for 3-4 minutes or until chicken is just cooked. Add mushrooms and cook, stirring, for 2 minutes longer.
2 Stir sour cream, tomato paste (pureé), paprika and black pepper to taste into pan, bring to simmering and simmer for 5 minutes or until sauce thickens. Sprinkle with spring onions or parsley and serve immediately.

Note: Chicken is a cheaper choice for protein and works just as well as red meat in classic dishes such as this. Serve with rice or pasta and a green salad. If you prefer a saucier mixture, add a little chicken stock or a 440g/14oz can of undrained mashed tomatoes at same time as the mushrooms.

Serves 6

green
chicken curry

Method:

1 *Heat oil in a wok over a medium heat, add onion, lemon grass and lime leaves and stir-fry for 3 minutes or until onion is golden.*

2 *Add curry paste and shrimp paste (if using) and stir-fry for 3 minutes longer or until fragrant. Stir in coconut milk, fish sauce and sugar, bring to the boil, then reduce heat and simmer, stirring frequently, for 10 minutes.*

3 *Add chicken, bamboo shoots, sweet corn and basil and cook, stirring frequently, for 15 minutes or until chicken is tender.*

Medium: *Fresh lemon grass is available from Oriental food shops and some supermarkets and greengrocers. It is also available dried; if using dried lemon grass soak it in hot water for 20 minutes or until soft before using. Lemon grass is also available in bottles from supermarkets, use this in the same way as you would fresh lemon grass.*

Serves 6

ingredients

**1 tablespoon peanut (groundnut) oil
1 onion, chopped
1 stalk fresh lemon grass, finely chopped or 1 teaspoon dried lemon grass, soaked in hot water until soft
3 kaffir lime leaves, finely shredded
2 tablespoons Thai green curry paste
1 teaspoon shrimp paste (optional)
2 cups/500ml/16fl oz coconut milk
1 tablespoon Thai fish sauce (nam pla)
1 tablespoon sugar
1 kg/2 lb boneless chicken thigh or breast fillets, cut into 2cm/³⁄₄in cubes
220g/7oz canned bamboo shoots, drained
31g/10oz canned baby sweet corn, drained
2 tablespoons chopped fresh basil**

green banana
chicken curry

Method:

1 Combine salt and turmeric and rub over bananas.

2 Heat oil in a wok over a medium heat, add bananas and stir-fry for 5 minutes or until brown. Remove bananas from pan and drain on absorbent kitchen paper.

3 Add spring onions, ginger and chillies to pan and stir-fry for 2 minutes or until mixture is soft. Stir in coconut milk, cinnamon, sultanas, cashews and chicken and bring to simmering. Simmer, stirring occasionally, for 20 minutes.

4 Slice bananas, return to pan and simmer, stirring occasionally, for 10 minutes or until chicken is tender. Remove cinnamon stick before serving.

Serves 6

ingredients

salt
1 teaspoon ground turmeric
10 green bananas, peeled
2 tablespoons vegetable oil
3 spring onions, chopped
1 tablespoon finely grated fresh ginger
2 small fresh red chillies,
seeded and chopped
1¹/₂ cups/375ml/12fl oz coconut milk
1 cinnamon stick
45g/1¹/₂oz sultanas
30g/1oz roasted cashews
6 chicken breast fillets, cut into
thin strips

chicken
and nut stirfry

Method:

1 To make sauce, place marmalade, stock and lime juice in a bowl and mix to combine. Set aside.

2 Heat oil in a wok over a medium heat, add onion and ginger and stir-fry for 3 minutes or until onion is golden. Increase heat to high, add chicken and stir-fry for 5 minutes or until chicken is brown. Remove chicken mixture from wok, set aside and keep warm.

3 Add pear to wok and stir-fry for 3 minutes or until golden. Return chicken mixture to wok, add sauce and stir-fry for 3 minutes or until sauce thickens slightly. Season to taste with black pepper. Scatter with nuts and coriander and serve immediately.

Note: This stir-fry can be made using other nut oils and nuts. You might like to try walnut oil and walnuts or almond oil and almonds. Nut oils are available from larger supermarkets and specialty delicatessens.

Serves 4

ingredients

I tablespoon macadamia or vegetable oil
I onion, cut into eighths
2 tablespoons finely grated fresh ginger
4 boneless chicken breast fillets, thinly sliced
I pear (peeled, cored and cut into thick slices)
freshly ground black pepper
60g/2oz macadamia or Brazil nuts, chopped
2 tablespoons fresh coriander (cilantro) leaves

Ginger lime sauce
I tablespoon ginger lime marmalade
1/2 cup/125ml/4fl oz chicken stock
I tablespoon lime juice

portuguese
chicken

Method:

1 Heat 2 tablespoons oil in a frying pan over a medium heat, add chicken and cook for 2-3 minutes each side or until brown. Remove chicken from pan and set aside.

2 Heat remaining oil in pan, add onions and cook, stirring, for 5 minutes or until golden. Add garlic and cook for 1 minute longer.

3 Return chicken to pan, add tomatoes, mushrooms, stock and tomato paste (purée) and bring to the boil. Reduce heat, cover and simmer for 30 minutes or until chicken is cooked. Season to taste with black pepper and sprinkle with parsley.

Note: For a complete meal serve on a bed of boiled white or brown rice. The cooking time will vary according to the size of the chicken thighs.

Serves 4

ingredients

4 tablespoons vegetable oil
8 chicken thighs, skinned and all visible fat removed
2 onions, diced
3 cloves garlic, crushed
440g/14oz canned tomatoes, drained and mashed
8 mushrooms, sliced
¹/₂ cup/125ml/4fl oz chicken stock
2 tablespoons tomato paste (purée)
freshly ground black pepper
2 tablespoons chopped fresh parsley

vineyard chicken

spring chicken

The freshness of spring arrives

and with it comes the availability of new season herbs, fruits and vegetables. Enjoy the temptations of Drumsticks in Dill Sauce, Chicken with Oregano and Lemon or Citrus and Spice Grilled Chicken.

vineyard
chicken

Photograph page 41

Method:

1 Make a deep slit in the side of each chicken fillet to form a pocket.
2 To make filling, place ricotta cheese, basil and black pepper to taste in a bowl and mix to combine. Fill pockets with filling and secure with toothpicks.
3 Heat oil in a large frying pan, add onions and garlic and cook, stirring, for 3 minutes or until onions are soft. Add tomatoes, green capsicum (pepper) and wine to pan and cook, stirring, for 2 minutes.
4 Add chicken to pan, cover and simmer, turning chicken occasionally, for 30 minutes or until chicken is tender.
Note: To serve six, increase the ingredients by half. This recipe can be completed to the end of step 2 several hours in advance.

Serves 4

ingredients

4 boneless chicken breast or thigh fillets
2 teaspoons vegetable oil
2 onions, sliced
2 cloves garlic, crushed
440g/14oz canned tomatoes, undrained and mashed
1 green capsicum (pepper), chopped
1 cup/250ml/4fl oz dry white wine

Ricotta filling
125g/4oz ricotta cheese, drained
2 tablespoons chopped fresh basil
freshly ground black pepper

chicken steaks
with herb sauce

Method:

1 Pound thigh fillets on both sides with a meat mallet to flatten.
2 Heat enough butter to coat base of a large heavy-based frying pan. Place thigh fillets in and cook 3 minutes on each side over medium heat. Remove to a heated plate.
3 Add garlic and onions and fry over gentle heat until onions are soft. Add salt, pepper, lemon juice and parsley. Stir quickly to lift pan juices and pour over chicken steaks. Serve immediately with vegetable accompaniments.
Serves 4

ingredients

500g/2lb chicken thigh fillets
1-2 tablespoons butter
1 clove garlic, finely chopped
1 medium onion, finely chopped
salt, pepper
1/4 cup/60ml/2fl oz lemon juice
1 tablespoon parsley, chopped

chicken
patties

Method:

1 *Mix all patty ingredients together and knead a little with one hand to distribute ingredients and make it fine in texture. Cover and rest in refrigerator for 20 minutes. With wet hands, form into small flat patties about 2½cm in diameter. Place on a flat tray until needed and refrigerate.*

2 *Prepare batter for flapjacks. Sift the flour, baking powder and salt into a bowl. Mix together the basil, garlic and milk, then beat in the egg. Make a well in the centre of the flour and pour in the milk mixture. Stir to form a smooth batter. Cover and set aside for 20 minutes.*

3 *Heat barbecue until hot and oil the grill bars and hotplate. Brush the patties with a little oil and place on grill bars. Grill for 2 minutes each side, cook the flapjacks at the same time, pour ¼ cup of mixture onto the greased hotplate. Cook until bubbles appear over the surface and the bottom is golden. Flip over with an eggslice and cook until golden. Transfer to a clean towel and cover to keep hot.*

4 *Serve a flapjack on each plate and arrange 3 patties on top with a dollop of chilli yoghurt sauce.*

5 *Serve with a side salad and the extra flapjacks.*

Serves 6

ingredients

Patties
500g/1 lb mince beef
½ teaspoon salt
¼ teaspoon pepper
1 teaspoon crushed garlic
2 tablespoons freshly chopped chilli
2 tablespoons dried breadcrumbs
¼ cup/60ml/2fl oz water

Flapjacks
1 cup/150g/5oz all purpose flour
1 teaspoon baking powder
¼ teaspoon salt
2 tablespoons freshly blended
basil and garlic
¾ cup/180ml/6fl oz milk
1 egg

Chilli Yoghurt Sauce
200g/7 oz natural yoghurt
1 tablespoon freshly chopped chilli
Mix yoghurt and chilli together

smoked
chicken salad

Method:
1 *Arrange chicken, capsicums (peppers), tomatoes and lettuce attractively in a salad bowl or on a serving platter.*
2 *To make dressing, place French dressing, mayonnaise, mustard and basil in a small bowl and mix to combine. Spoon dressing over salad and serve immediately.*

Serving suggestion: *Accompany with toasted rye or wholemeal bread.*

Note: *Smoked chicken is one of the more recent food products and is available from some supermarkets and delicatessens. It has been cured and smoked and has a pale pink flesh with a delicate flavour.*

Serves 4

ingredients

1¹/₂kg/3 lb smoked chicken, skin removed and flesh shredded
2 red capsicums (peppers), roasted and cut into thin strips
2 yellow capsicums (peppers), roasted and cut into thin strips
2 green capsicums (peppers), roasted and cut into thin strips
250g/8oz cherry tomatoes, halved
1 cos lettuce, leaves separated and torn into pieces

Basil dressing
3 tablespoons French dressing
¹/₂ cup/125 g/4 oz mayonnaise
1 tablespoon wholegrain mustard
2 tablespoons chopped fresh basil

southern-fried
chicken drumsticks

Method:

1 Rinse drumsticks and pat dry with paper towel. Smooth the skin over the drumstick if needed.

2 Mix flour, salt and pepper, place on paper-lined, flat plate. Beat eggs and milk well together in a deep plate.

3 Dip the drumsticks in the flour then into the egg, turning to coat both sides. Place again into the flour, lift end of paper to toss flour over drumstick and roll in flour until well covered. Place in single layer on a clean, flat tray.

4 Heat oil in a large frying pan. Add drumsticks and fry a few minutes on each side until just beginning to colour. Reduce heat, place a lid on the pan and cook slowly for 20 minutes, turning chicken after 10 minutes.

5 Remove lid and increase heat, continue cooking until golden brown and crisp, turning frequently. Remove from pan, drain on paper towels. Serve hot with vegetable accompaniments.

Serves 4

ingredients

1kg/2 lb chicken drumsticks
1¹/₂ cups/180g/6fl oz flour
1 teaspoon salt and pepper
2 eggs
¹/₃ cup/80ml/3fl oz milk
¹/₂ cup/120ml/4fl oz canola oil

drumsticks
in dill sauce

Method:

1 Heat butter in a wide-based saucepan. Add drumsticks a few at a time and brown lightly on all sides. Remove to a plate and brown remainder.

2 Add shallots and sauté for one minute. Stir in chopped dill. Add lemon juice, return drumsticks to saucepan, sprinkle with salt and pepper.

3 Arrange the carrots over the drumsticks. Add water and stock cube. Bring to a simmer, turn down heat, cover and simmer for 40 minutes until tender.

4 Remove drumsticks and carrots with a slotted spoon and arrange on a heated platter. Blend the cornflour with water, stir into the juices remaining in the pan. Stir over heat until sauce boils and thickens. Pour over drumsticks and carrots. Serve immediately with crusty bread.

Serves 6

ingredients

2 tablespoons butter
1 kg/2lb chicken drumsticks
1 cup/45g/1¹/₂oz chopped shallots
3 tablespoons finely chopped dill
¹/₄ cup/60g/2fl oz lemon juice
¹/₂ teaspoon salt
¹/₄ teaspoon white pepper
1 bunch Dutch carrots, peeled
2 cups/500ml/16fl oz water
1 chicken stock cube
2 tablespoons cornflour
2 tablespoons water

rice
with chicken livers

Method:

1 *Wash chicken livers, and remove any sinew. Chop livers into bite-size pieces.*

2 *Heat butter in a large saucepan and sauté the shallots for five minutes until tender. Add the chicken livers, and cook for a further few minutes until they change colour.*

3 *Add the rice and chicken stock to the saucepan, bring to the boil, then simmer with the lid on, stirring occasionally, for approximately 30 minutes, until the liquid has been absorbed and the rice is cooked. If the rice is not cooked and the mixture is looking a little dry, add a further cup of water, and cook for a further five minutes.*

4 *When rice is cooked, toss the chopped parsley, pinenuts and currants through the rice, and serve.*

Serves 8

ingredients

1kg/2 lb chicken livers
75g/2¹⁄₂oz butter
12 shallots, chopped
375g/1¹⁄₂ cups short grain rice
2¹⁄₂cups/600ml/20fl oz chicken stock
1 bunch parsley, chopped
100g/3oz pine nuts
100g/3oz currants

chicken
with oregano and lemon

Method:

1 Season chicken with dried oregano, pepper and salt.
2 Heat oil in a large fry pan.
3 Add chicken, potatoes and onions, and brown quickly for 2-3 minutes.
4 Pour in stock, cover, and simmer for 10-15 minutes or until chicken is cooked.
5 Add lemon juice and fresh oregano. Season to taste. Cook for a further three minutes. Serve immediately.

ingredients

**4 chicken breasts
2 teaspoons dried oregano
freshly ground pepper and salt
2 tablespoons olive oil
600g/20oz potatoes, sliced to
5mm/¹/sin
I bunch spring onions, trimmed and
halved
125ml/4fl oz chicken stock
75ml/2¹/₂fl oz lemon juice
2 sprigs oregano, chopped
salt and pepper to taste**

chicken
with ricotta, rocket & roasted red (pepper) capsicum

Method:

1 *Preheat the oven to 200°C/400°F.*
2 *Combine ricotta, rocket, pinenuts, capsicum (pepper), and pepper & salt in a small bowl, and mix together until smooth.*
3 *Place 1-2 tablespoons of ricotta mixture under the skin of each chicken breast. Lightly grease a baking dish. Place the chicken breasts in the dish, sprinkle with pepper & salt, place 1 teaspoon butter on each breast, pour stock around the chicken, and bake for 20-25 minutes.*
4 *Serve chicken with pan-juices and a rocket salad.*

Serves 4

ingredients

200g/7oz fresh ricotta
1 bunch rocket, roughly chopped
¹/₄ cup/30g/1oz pinenuts, toasted
¹/₂ red capsicum (pepper), roasted
and finely chopped
freshly ground pepper & salt
4 chicken breasts with skin on;
each around 200g/7oz
1 tablespoon butter
250ml/8fl oz chicken stock

chicken
with basil cream sauce

Method:

1 Combine the flour, pepper & salt in a bowl and coat the chicken evenly with the flour, shaking off the excess.

2 Heat oil and butter in a pan, add the chicken, and cook over medium heat for 5-6 minutes each side. Remove from the pan and keep warm.

3 Basil Cream Sauce: Wipe out the pan, heat the butter, add the garlic and cook for 2 minutes. Add chicken stock, cream and lemon juice, bring to boil and reduce a little.

4 Just before serving, add the basil season with pepper & salt, and serve the sauce with the chicken.

Serves 4

ingredients

4 chicken breasts each 200g/7oz
3 tablespoons flour
freshly ground pepper & salt
1 tablespoon olive oil
1 tablespoon butter

Basil Cream Sauce
1 tablespoon butter
2 cloves garlic, crushed
1/2 cup/125ml/4fl oz chicken stock
1/2 cup/125ml/4fl oz cream
65ml/2oz cup lemon juice
2 tablespoons basil, finely chopped
freshly ground pepper
sea salt

citrus & spice
grilled chicken

Method:

1 Wash chicken inside and out and pat dry with paper towels. With a cleaver or large sharp knife, cut chicken through the breastbone and open out. Cut on each side of the backbone and discard. (May be used for stock).

2 Mix marinade ingredients together. Place chicken halves in a non-metal dish and smother with the marinade. Cover and refrigerate for 12 hours or overnight, turning occasionally.

3 Heat oven griller element or gas griller to medium. Place chicken halves in the base of the grill pan under the grill. Cook for 10 minutes on each side brushing frequently with marinade.

4 Lift chicken onto grilling rack so as to come closer to heat, cook 5 minutes on each side. Turn heat to high and cook about 2 minutes to brown and crisp. Remove chicken to a heated platter.

5 Skim the fat from the pan juices and pour juices over the chicken. Serve hot with vegetable accompaniments.

ingredients

1 kg/2lb whole chicken

For marinade
¹/₂ cup/120ml/4fl oz cider vinegar
¹/₂ cup/120ml/4fl oz orange juice
¹/₂ cup/120ml/4fl oz grapefruit juice
1 teaspoon cinnamon
¹/₂ teaspoon ground nutmeg
1 teaspoon sugar
¹/₂ teaspoon salt (optional)

Serves 2-3

oven baked
chicken schnitzels

Method:

1 Place each chicken fillet between 2 pieces plastic wrap and flatten to even thinness with the side of a meat mallet or rolling pin. Place on a platter. Mix the salt, pepper, lemon juice and chilli sauce togethe and pour over the chicken. Cover and refrigerate for 20 minutes.

2 Spread flour onto a sheet of kitchen paper. Beat eggs with one tablespoon water and place in a shallow tray or dish. Spread breadcrumbs onto a sheet of kitchen paper. Coat each side of chicken fillets in flour, (shake off excess) then egg, and press into the breadcrumbs to coat both sides. Place on a flat surface in single layer. Lightly spray schnitzels with canola oil spray.

3 Place oiled side down on a rack over an oven tray (a cake-rack is suitable). Lightly spray top-side with canola oil spray. Place in a preheated oven (180°C/350°F) and cook for 8 minutes, turn with tongs and cook for a further 8 minutes.

4 Serve with vegetable accompaniments or a salad.

ingredients

1kg/2lb tray chicken breast
fillets (skin off)
salt, pepper
juice of 1 lemon
2 tablespoons sweet chilli sauce
³/₄ cup/90g/3oz flour
2 eggs
1¹/₂ cups/180g/6fl oz dried
breadcrumbs
canola oil spray

52

Serves 5-6

chicken
and avocado focaccia

Method:

1 *To make salsa, place avocado, coriander (cilantro), lime or lemon juice, mayonnaise and chilli in a bowl and mix gently to combine. Set aside.*

2 *Heat oil in a frying pan over a medium heat, add chicken, paprika and cumin and cook, stirring, for 5 minutes or until chicken is tender.*

3 *Top focaccia bases with chicken mixture, cheese and cucumber. Spoon over salsa and top with remaining focaccia halves. Serve immediately.*

Note: *A combination of chopped fresh chives and mint may be used instead of the coriander.*

Serves 4

ingredients

2 teaspoons vegetable oil
2 boneless chicken breast fillets, sliced
1 teaspoon paprika
1 teaspoon ground cumin
4 x 12cm/5in focaccia squares, split
and toasted
4 slices Swiss cheese
¹/₂ cucumber, sliced

Avocado salsa
1 avocado, stoned, peeled and mashed
2 tablespoons chopped fresh coriander
(cilantro)
2 tablespoons lime or lemon juice
2 tablespoons mayonnaise
1 fresh red chilli, chopped

thigh steaks in fruity mint salsa

sizzling
summer

The tastes of summer....

a light and refreshing salad accompanied by the fragrant smell of perfectly barbecued chicken. Nothing else inspires us more than the combination of cooking, the great outdoors and friends.

thigh steaks
in fruity mint salsa

Photograph page 55

Method:

1 *Pound thigh fillets on both sides with a meat mallet to flatten. Sprinkle with salt (if using), pepper and oregano.*
2 *Heat a non-stick frying pan and lightly spray with oil, place in the thigh steaks and cook for 3 minutes on each side. Remove to a heated plate and keep hot.*
3 *Add diced pear, banana, lemon juice, mint and chilli sauce to the pan. Scrape up pan juices and stir to heat fruit.*
4 *Pile hot fruit salsa on top of thigh steaks. Serve immediately with mashed potatoes or rice.*

Serves 3-4

ingredients

500g/1 lb chicken thighs
canola oil spray
salt, pepper to taste (optional)
1/2 teaspoon dried oregano
1 pear, peeled and diced
1 banana, peeled and diced
2 tablespoons lemon juice
3 tablespoons finely chopped mint
2 teaspoons sweet chilli sauce

honey balsamic
barbequed drumsticks

Method:

1 *Rinse and dry drumsticks with paper towel. Place in a single layer in a non-metal dish. Mix honey, vinegar, ginger, salt and pepper together and pour over drumsticks. Stand 1 hour or longer in refrigerator.*
2 *Heat barbecue or grill until hot. Place a wire cake rack over barbecue grill bars and lightly oil. Arrange drumsticks on rack and cook 20-25 minutes, turning frequently and brushing with honey mixture. For gas or electric grill place in base of grill tray.*
3 *Remove cake-rack from barbecue and transfer drumsticks directly onto grill bars, or elevate drumsticks onto the pan grilling rack under the grill. Cook approximately 5-10 minutes more until brown and crisp, turning occasionally. Serve hot with salads.*

ingredients

1kg/2lb chicken drumsticks
1/2 cup/120g/4oz honey
3 tablespoons balsamic vinegar
2 teaspoons fresh ginger juice
or 1/2 teaspoon ground ginger
salt, pepper to taste

Tip: *The drumsticks cook perfectly in an upright griller. Set griller to moderate for first 20 minutes then increase heat to high. Baste as directed but there is no need to turn.*

Serves 4-5

southern
barbequed chicken

Method:

1 Prepare the Southern Barbecue Sauce in advance. Place all ingredients into a stainless steel saucepan, stir to combine. Bring to a simmer and continue to simmer over low heat for 15-20 minutes, stirring regularly to prevent from catching. Stand for 1 hour to cook and to allow flavours to blend. Store in jars or bottles in the refrigerator if not to be used immediately.

2 Cut chicken into pieces. As 2kg/4lb is a large bird, the breast may be cut into 3 or 4 pieces each side.

3 Heat barbecue to moderate and oil the grill plate. Lightly sear chicken pieces on all sides over direct heat about 4 minutes each side. Lift the chicken onto a plate.

4 Place 1 1/2 cups of the sauce into a bowl and place by the barbecue. Place a sheet of baking paper over the grill bars and prick at intervals between the runs to allow ventilation. Place the chicken onto the baking paper and brush well with the sauce.

5 Close the lid and cook for 10 minutes, then lift the lid, brush with sauce, turn chicken, brush underside with sauce, close lid and cook 10 minutes. Repeat this process every 10 minutes, a total of approximately 4-5 times or for 40-50 minutes until chicken is rich brown in colour and cooked through. If chicken is cooking too quickly, reduce heat by turning down gas or rake the coals to the sides. Heat extra sauce in a small saucepan on the barbecue.

6 Serve chicken with hot sauce and jacket potatoes cooked on the barbecue with the chicken. Accompany with a salad.

Note: This is best cooked on a charcoal or gas barbecue with a lid or hood.

Serves 6-8

ingredients

1 x 2kg/4lb chicken, cut into pieces
Southern Barbecue Sauce
350ml/12oz can tomato puree
1 cup/240ml/8fl oz cider vinegar
1/2 cup/120ml/4fl oz canola oil
1/3 cup/80ml/2 1/2oz Worcestershire sauce
1/2 cup/75g/2 1/2oz brown sugar
1/4 cup/60g/2oz golden syrup or molasses
2 tablespoons French-style mustard
2-3 cloves garlic, crushed
1/4 cup/60ml/2fl oz lemon juice
1 x 2kg/4lb chicken, cut into pieces

char-grilled
tarragon chicken

Method:

1 Place chicken in a single layer in a shallow glass or ceramic dish. Combine tarragon, wine, lemon rind and green peppercorns. Pour marinade over chicken. Turn to coat chicken with marinade and marinate at room temperature, turning once, for 20 minutes.

2 Remove chicken from marinade and cook on a preheated hot char grill or in a preheated grill pan for 5 minutes or until tender.
Note: Do not marinate chicken any longer than 20 minutes as the marinade will cause the chicken to break down. As an alternative to cooking the chicken on a char grill you can cook it under a preheated hot grill.

ingredients

6 boneless chicken breast fillets, skin removed
3 tablespoons chopped fresh tarragon or 2 teaspoons dried tarragon
I cup/250ml/8fl oz dry white wine
2 tablespoons lemon rind strips
I tablespoon green peppercorns in brine, drained and crushed

Serves 6

spicy
mango chicken

Method:

1 *Preheat barbecue to a high heat. Place chicken between sheets of greaseproof paper and pound lightly with a meat mallet to flatten to 1 cm/¹/₂in thick.*

2 *Combine black pepper, cumin and paprika and sprinkle over chicken. Layer prosciutto or ham and mango slices on chicken, roll up and secure with wooden toothpicks or cocktail sticks. Place chicken on lightly oiled barbecue and cook for 3-5 minutes each side or until chicken is tender and cooked.*

3 *To make sauce, place mango, garlic, golden syrup and chilli sauce in a small saucepan and cook, stirring, over a low heat for 4-5 minutes or until sauce thickens slightly. Serve with chicken.*

Note: *Drained, canned mangoes can be used in place of fresh. You will need two 440g/14oz cans of mangoes. Use three-quarters of one can for the sauce and the remainder for the filling in the chicken.*

Serves 4

ingredients

4 boneless chicken breast fillets
1 teaspoon freshly ground
black pepper
1 teaspoon ground cumin
1 teaspoon paprika
4 slices prosciutto or ham, halved
2 mangoes, peeled and cut
into 2cm/³/₄in thick slices

Mango sauce
1 mango, peeled and chopped
1 clove garlic, crushed
2 tablespoons golden syrup
1 tablespoon sweet chilli sauce

thai
lime spatchcocks

Method:

1 *Cut spatchcocks (poussins) down middle of backs and flatten. Thread a skewer through wings and a skewer through legs of each spatchcock.*

2 *To make marinade, place lime juice, coriander, coconut milk, chilli, honey, and black pepper to taste in a large baking dish. Mix to combine. Place spatchcocks flesh side down in marinade. Cover and refrigerate for 4 hours or overnight.*

3 *Cook on a hot barbecue or under a hot grill, basting frequently with marinade. Cook 15 minutes each side, or until tender and cooked through.*

ingredients

4 small spatchcocks (poussins)

Marinade
3 tablespoons lime juice
2 tablespoons chopped fresh coriander (cilanto)
1 cup/250ml/8fl oz coconut milk
1 red chilli, chopped
2 tablespoons honey
freshly ground black pepper

Serves 4

skewered
chicken livers with coriander

Method:
1 Place coriander pesto, crushed garlic, chopped ginger, oil and lemon juice in a bowl.
   Cut chicken livers into 2 through centre membrane and carefully stir into the coriander marinade. Cover and refrigerate for 1 hour or more.
2 Cut each bacon strip into 3 approximately 10cm/4in strips. Wrap a strip of bacon around each halved liver and secure with a toothpick.
3 Heat the barbecue until hot. Place on overturned wire cake-rack over the grill bars. Arrange the skewered livers on the rack. Cook for 8-10 minutes, turning frequently and brushing with any remaining marinade. Serve as finger food.
   Note: Cook on any flat-top barbecue or electric barbecue grill.

ingredients

2 tablespoons of coriander
with Fetta cheese pesto
1 teaspoon crushed garlic
1 teaspoon chopped ginger
2 teaspoons oil
1 tablespoon lemon juice
250g/8oz chicken livers
6 rashers bacon
toothpicks

**Yields approximately
22 skewers**

chicken
and mushroom kebabs

Method:
1 Place lime or lemon juice, oil and chilli powder in a bowl and mix to combine. Add chicken and mushroom halves and toss to combine. Set aside to marinate for 30 minutes.
2 Preheat barbecue to a high heat. Drain chicken and mushrooms, reserving marinade. Thread a chicken cube and a mushroom half onto each bamboo skewer. Brush with reserved marinade and cook on lightly oiled barbecue, turning several times, for 4-5 minutes or until chicken is cooked.

ingredients

1 tablespoon lime or lemon juice
1 tablespoon vegetable oil
1 pinch chilli powder
1 chicken breast fillet, skin removed, cut into 10 cubes
5 button mushrooms, halved

Serves 4

chicken
caesar salad

Method:

1 Trim the chicken fillets. Mix together the garlic, salt, pepper, oil and lemon juice. Cover and marinate the chicken for 30 minutes in the refrigerator.

2 Heat grill or chargrill until hot. Sear the fillets one minute on each side, then cook 3 minutes each side. Remove and rest for 5 minutes before cutting into $^1/_2$cm slices on the diagonal.

3 Separate the leaves of the cos lettuce, discard outer leaves and wash well. Drain and shake dry in a clean tea towel. Cut greener leaves into bite-sized pieces and leave the pale inner leaves whole. Cover and place in refrigerator until ready for use.

4 Place the anchovy in base of the salad bowl and mash with the back of a fork while the oil is being added. Gradually add the lemon juice while beating, and sprinkle in the salt and pepper. Break in the coddled egg, scraping the set white from inside the shell and lightly stir. Add the mustard and Worcestershire sauce.

5 Add the cos lettuce leaves; toss to coat lightly with dressing while sprinkling over the grated Parmesan cheese. Toss in the chicken and croutons. Rearrange the whole leaves to stand upright and garnish with shaved Parmesan cheese. Serve immediately.

Tip: To make croutons. Use unsliced day-old white bread. Cut slices $1^1/_2$cm thick, remove crusts and cut into $1^1/_2$cm cubes. Peel 2 cloves garlic and cut in half. Add enough oil to be $^1/_2$cm deep in the frying pan, add garlic and heat. Remove garlic when golden; add bread cubes, stir and toss as they fry to golden colour. Remove quickly from pan and drain on paper towels.

To coddle egg. Bring the egg to room temperature. Boil water in a small saucepan and when it reaches the boil, turn heat off and immediately lower in the egg.

ingredients

2 chicken breast fillets
1 clove garlic, crushed
salt and pepper
2 teaspoons olive oil
1 tablespoon lemon juice
1 cos lettuce

Dressing
2 anchovy fillets
4 tablespoons olive oil
$2^1/_2$ tablespoons lemon juice
$^1/_2$ teaspoon salt
$^1/_4$ teaspoon pepper
1 coddled egg
pinch of dry mustard
1 teaspoon Worcestershire sauce
1 cup/60g/2oz garlic croutons
$^1/_4$ cup/30g/1oz grated Parmesan cheese
shaved Parmesan cheese for garnish

Stand for 1 minute in the water. If egg is cold from refrigerator allow $1^1/_2$ minutes.

Tip: To joint a chicken: Remove leg and thigh at the joint. Separate the leg and thigh cutting through the joint. Remove wings at the joint. Cut the breast from the back bone along the fine rib bones an each side. Cut through the centre breast bone. Cut each breast into 2 pieces.

Serves 5

teriyaki
tenderloins

Method:

1 *Place tenderloins in a non-metal container and stir in about ³/₄ cup Teriyaki marinade. Cover and marinate for 30 minutes at room temperature or several hours or overnight in the refrigerator.*

2 *Heat the barbecue until hot. Place a sheet of baking paper over the grill bars and make a few slits between the bars for ventilation, or place baking paper on the hot plate. Place the tenderloins on grill and cook for 2 minutes on each side until cooked through and golden. Brush with marinade as they cook. Serve immediately with extra Teriyaki marinade as a dipping sauce.*

Serves 4

ingredients

500g/1 lb chicken tenderloins
375g/12¹/₂oz bottle Teriyaki marinade

Serving Suggestions:

1 *Serve with steamed rice and vegetables.*

2 *Toss into salad greens to make a hot salad. Dress salad with 1 tablespoon Teriyaki marinade, 1 tablespoon vinegar and 3 tablespoons salad oil.*

3 *Stuff into heated pocket breads along with shredded lettuce, cucumber and onion rings and drizzle with an extra spoonful of Teriyaki marinade.*

lemon barbecue
roasted chicken with vegetables

Method:

1 *Wash chicken inside and out, drain then pat dry with paper towels.*

2 *Wash lemons then peel off the zest with a potato peeler. Dice the zest finely. Juice the lemons. Mix together half of the lemon zest, lemon juice, garlic, salt, pepper, oregano and oil.*

3 *Stand the chicken in a dish and spoon half of the lemon mixture over the chicken and in the cavity. Place remaining zest in the cavity.*

4 *Prepare fire for the kettle barbecue for indirect heat according to manufacturer's instructions or preheat gas barbecue. Place chicken directly onto oiled grill over direct heat and sear on all sides. Move to indirect heat over dripping pan.*

5 *Place potatoes and pumpkin in 2 foil trays; sprinkle with remaining lemon mixture, tossing around to coat all pieces. Place trays over direct heat. Cover barbecue with lid or hood and cook for 1 to 1½ hours, brushing chicken with lemon and herb mixture every 20 minutes. Turn vegetables.*

6 *Remove vegetables when cooked, cover to keep hot. Rest chicken for 5 minutes before carving. Serve hot with roasted vegetables and a side salad.*

Serves 4

ingredients

1 x 1.8kg/4lb chicken
2 lemons
2 cloves garlic, crushed
salt, pepper
2 teaspoons chopped fresh oregano
2 tablespoons olive oil

Vegetables
4 medium-sized brown potatoes, peeled and quartered
500g/1 lb pumpkin cut into portions (skin on)

chicken
and fresh herb terrine

Photograph opposite

ingredients

1 bunch/500g/1 lb spinach or silverbeet
250g/8oz chicken livers, cleaned
1 tablespoon seasoned flour
15g/1oz butter
1 teaspoon olive oil
375g/12oz chicken meat, a mixture of
white and dark meat, minced
375g/12oz lean pork, minced
2 teaspoons finely chopped fresh
thyme or 1 teaspoon dried thyme
3 cloves garlic, crushed
2 onions, diced
1 tablespoon green peppercorns in
brine, drained
3 eggs
1/2 cup/125ml/4fl oz dry white wine
2 tablespoons port or sherry
3 tablespoons chopped fresh parsley
freshly ground black pepper

Method:

1 *Pre-heat oven to 180°C/350°F.*

2 *Boil, steam or microwave spinach or silverbeet leaves to soften. Drain; refresh under cold running water and drain again. Line a lightly greased terrine dish or an 11 x 21cm/4¹/2 x 8¹/2 in loaf tin with overlapping spinach leaves. Allow leaves to overhang the sides.*

3 *Toss chicken livers in seasoned flour to coat. Heat butter and oil in a frying pan over a medium heat until foaming. Add chicken livers and cook, stirring, for 3-5 minutes or until they just change colour. Remove livers from pan and set aside to cool.*

4 *Chop chicken livers. Place chicken livers, chicken, pork, thyme, garlic, onions, green peppercorns, eggs, wine, port or sherry, parsley and black pepper to taste in a bowl and mix to combine.*

5 *Pack meat mixture into prepared terrine dish or loaf tin, fold overhanging spinach leaves over filling and cover with aluminium foil. Place terrine dish of loaf in a baking dish with enough boiling water to come halfway up the sides of the dish and bake for 2 hours. Drain off any juices, cover top of terrine with foil, then weight and set aside to cool. When cold refrigerate overnight. To serve, unmould and cut into slices.*

Note: *The terrine will improve if kept for 1-2 days before serving. Accompanied by a tossed salad of watercress of rocket, a bowl of gherkins and some French bread this makes a truly delicious starter or light meal.*

Serves 10

marinated
chicken and pear salad

Method:

1 *Remove the flesh from the chicken. Carve chicken and discard the bones. Place chicken in a flat, non-metal dish and place dried pears on top.*
2 *Mix marinade ingredients together, pour over chicken and pears and refrigerate for 2 hours.*
3 *Place salad greens on serving plate, arrange the chicken strips and pear halves on the salad.*
4 *Whisk the remaining marinade with a little extra oil and spoon over the salad.*

Serves 6-8

ingredients

1 x 1.5kg/3lb chicken (oven barbecued)
200g/7oz packet dried pears

Marinade
¹/₂ cup/120ml/4fl oz olive oil
¹/₂ cup/120ml/4fl oz orange juice
2 tablespoons red wine vinegar
3 whole cloves
3 small bay leaves
2 tablespoons pine nuts
¹/₄ cup/45g/1¹/₄oz raisins
1 teaspoon sweet chilli sauce

Salad
500g/1 lb mixed salad greens, crisped
2 Lebanese cucumbers, thinly sliced
1 small spanish onion

chicken kebabs
with yoghurt and lemon sauce

Method:

1 Soak satay sticks in cold water for 30 minutes.
2 Place yoghurt, garlic, paprika, cummin seeds, lemon juice, parsley, oregano and pepper in a bowl, and mix until combined.
3 Place chicken on satay sticks and brush-over with half the mixture. Leave to marinate in refrigerator for 2-3 hours.
4 Heat oil on barbecue (or chargrill pan), add chicken kebabs and cook 4-5 minutes each side.
5 Serve with remaining marinade mixture.

Serves 4

ingredients

6 chicken thigh fillets, cubed
300g/10oz plain yoghurt
2 clove garlic, crushed
1 1/2 teaspoon paprika, ground
1 1/2 teaspoon cummin seeds
60ml/2oz lemon juice
2 tablespoons parsley, chopped
2 teaspoons oregano, chopped
freshly ground pepper
24 satay sticks

grilled
chicken salad

Method:

1 *Place coriander, chilli, soy sauce and lime juice in a bowl and mix to combine. Add chicken, toss to coat and marinate at room temperature for 30 minutes.*

2 *Preheat barbecue to a medium heat. Arrange rocket or watercress, tomatoes, feta cheese and olives attractively on a serving platter. Set aside.*

3 *To make dressing, place oil, lime juice and black pepper to taste in a screwtop jar and shake well to combine. Set aside.*

4 *Drain chicken, place on lightly oiled barbecue grill and cook for 4-5 minutes each side or until cooked through. Slice chicken, arrange on salad, drizzle with dressing and serve immediately.*

Note: *The chicken will come to no harm if marinated for longer than 30 minutes, but if you think the marinating will exceed 1 hour it is safer to place it in the refrigerator. When entertaining, this recipe can be prepared to the end of step 3 several hours in advance, then cover and store in the refrigerator until required.*

Serves 4

ingredients

**2 tablespoons chopped fresh coriander
(cilantro)
1 fresh red chilli, chopped
2 tablespoons soy sauce
2 tablespoons lime juice
4 boneless chicken breast fillets
1 bunch rocket or watercress
250g/8oz cherry tomatoes, halved
155g/5oz feta cheese, crumbled
90g/3oz marinated olives**

**<u>Lime dressing</u>
2 tablespoons olive oil
2 tablespoons lime juice
freshly ground black pepper**

chicken
pesto burgers

Method:

1 Preheat barbecue to a medium heat. To make patties, place basil leaves, pine nuts, Parmesan cheese, garlic and oil in a food processor or blender and process until smooth. Transfer mixture to a bowl, add chicken, breadcrumbs, red capsicum (pepper), onion, egg white and black pepper to taste and mix well to combine.

2 Shape chicken mixture into four patties. Place patties on lightly oiled barbecue plate (griddle) and cook for 3 minutes each side or until cooked.

3 To serve, top bottom half of each roll with rocket or watercress, then with a pattie, tomato slices and top half of roll. Serve immediately.

Note: Capsicums (peppers) are easy to roast on the barbecue. Remove seeds cut into quarters and place skin side down on a preheated hot barbecue. Cook until skins are charred and blistered, then place in a plastic food bag or paper bag and set aside until cool enough to handle. Remove skin and use as desired.

ingredients

4 rolls, slit and toasted
125g/4oz rocket or watercress
1 tomato, sliced

Chicken pesto patties
1/2 bunch fresh basil
2 tablespoons pine nuts
1 tablespoon grated Parmesan cheese
1 clove garlic, crushed
2 tablespoons olive oil
500g/1 lb chicken mince
1 cup/60g/2oz breadcrumbs, made from stale bread
1 red capsicum (pepper), roasted and diced
1 onion, diced
1 egg white
freshly ground black pepper

Serves 4

barbecued
spatchcocks

Method:

1 Preheat barbecue to a medium heat.
2 Place spatchcocks (poussins) on oiled barbecue grill and cook for 6-7 minutes each side or until tender and cooked through.
3 To make dressing, place olives, parsley, anchovies, garlic, vinegar, oil and black pepper to taste in a bowl and mix to combine. Spoon dressing over spatchcocks (poussins) and serve immediately.

Serves 6

ingredients

6 spatchcocks (poussins), halved and backbones removed

Green olive dressing
75g/2¹/₂oz green olives, pitted and finely chopped
4 tblspns chopped fresh flat-leaf parsley
2 canned anchovy fillets, chopped
I clove garlic, crushed
¹/₄ cup/60ml/2fl oz red wine vinegar
2 tablespoons olive oil
freshly ground pepper

spiced
chicken burgers

Method:

1 Preheat barbecue to a medium heat.
2 To make marinade, place yoghurt, coriander, curry paste, chutney and lemon juice in a shallow dish and mix to combine. Add chicken breasts, turn to coat and marinate for 20 minutes.
3 To make raita, cut cucumber in half, lengthwise and scrape out seeds. Cut cucumber into fine slices and place in a bowl. Add yoghurt, garlic and lemon juice and mix to combine. Cover and chill until ready to serve.
4 Drain chicken and cook on oiled barbecue grill for 4 minutes each side or until tender and cooked through. To serve, place chicken fillets on four pieces of bread, then top with tomatoes and raita and remaining pieces of bread.

Note: Turkish bread (pide) is a flat white leavened bread similar to Italian flatbread. It is usually baked in ovals measuring 30-40cm/12-16in. If Turkish bread is unavailable, country-style Italian bread, rye bread, sourdough, ciabatta or focaccia are all good alternatives for this recipe.

Makes 4 burgers

4 boneless chicken breast fillets
4 pieces Turkish (pide) bread, halved
4 tomatoes, sliced

Spiced yoghurt marinade
$^1/_2$ cup/100g/3$^1/_2$oz natural yoghurt
4 tablespoons chopped fresh coriander
2 tablespoons mild red curry paste
2 tablespoons mango chutney
2 tablespoons lemon juice

Cucumber raita
1 cucumber
1 cup/200g/6$^1/_2$oz thick natural yoghurt
1 clove garlic, crushed
1 tablespoon lemon juice

chicken
pineapple kebabs

Photograph opposite

Method:

1 Bring a medium saucepan of water to the boil, add the pumpkin and cook for 3 minutes, then drain.

2 Thread the chicken cubes, one pineapple cube and one pumpkin cube onto each skewer.

3 Brush chicken with the combined garlic, soy sauce, lemon juice and honey and grill under moderate heat or on a barbecue plate for about 3 minutes each side or until cooked through.

Serves 4

ingredients

**4 chicken breast fillets,
cut into 2cm/³/₄in cubes
200g/7oz pineapple,
cut into 2cm/³/₄in cubes
200g/7oz pumpkin,
cut into 2cm/³/₄in cubes
8 wooded skewers, soaked
2 cloves garlic, crushed
2 tablespoons soy sauce
4 tablespoons freshly squeezed
lemon juice
1 tablespoon honey**

sweet chicken
drumsticks with polenta crust

Photograph opposite

Method:

1 Brush each drumstick with the jam, then roll in the flour. Coat with the beaten eggs, then roll in the combined extra flour, salt and polenta, and coat well.

2 Deep-fry drumsticks until golden and cooked through (about 20 minutes).

Serves 4

ingredients

**8 chicken drumsticks
¹/₄ cup/60g/2oz apricot jam (jelly)
1 cup/120g/4oz plain flour
2 eggs, beaten
¹/₂ cup/60g/2oz flour, extra
1 tablespoon salt
³/₄ cup/90g/3oz polenta (cornmeal)
oil for deep-frying**

soup
& stocks

Chicken stock is the rich, flavoursome liquid obtained by slowly simmering chicken pieces, bones or a boiler chicken in water, with celery, carrot and onion added for extra flavour if desired. It is used as a base for soups, sauces, stews and casseroles and small quantities are used in stir-fry dishes. It is therefore handy to always have some in the freezer for the various cooking needs. A recipe for chicken stock is included in this section.

Helpful tips:

- Bags of chicken bones and carcasses may be bought for very little cost. Rinse well and break the carcasses so they will flatten. A combination of bones and a few chicken pieces, particularly wings and thigh pieces make a richer stock. Collect wing tips, chicken trimmings, bones and chicken neck, place in a plastic freezer bag and freeze. When enough is collected, proceed to make stock.
- Place the bones, trimming or pieces in a large saucepan and add enough cold water to cover the chicken by 5cm/2in. The amount will depend on the amount of bones and chicken pieces; too much water will result in a weaker stock, or extravagance of fuel until the excess water evaporates off. Bring stock slowly to simmering point over low heat to allow the extraction of the juices. Skim off the scum as it rises with a slotted spoon to remove impurities.
- Add salt, carrot, celery and onion cut into large pieces, as small pieces will pulp and cloud the stock. Avoid using starchy vegetables such as potato, peas, sweet potato, as they can also cloud the stock.

Also avoid strongly flavoured vegetables such as cabbage and cauliflower. Add bay leaf, sprig of thyme and parsley, or a bouquet garni sachet and peppercorns. Simmer uncovered for 45 minutes for small quantities or 1½-2 hours for large quantities or until the stock is rich in flavour.

- Strain the stock into a clean container. If it is to be used immediately, blot the surface with absorbent paper to remove the fat, otherwise refrigerate for 1 hour, then lift off the solidified fat from the surface. Place into covered containers and freeze. Freeze some stock in small lots to have ready for gravy, sauces and stir-fry.
- Fresh stock may be stored in the refrigerator for 4 days and in the freezer for 3-4 months.

Simple Soups and Sauces
Light Noodle Soup
Bring to a slow boil 1½ cups of chicken stock, crumble in 1 coil of egg noodles and cook for 10 minutes. A teaspoonful of tomato paste or a chopped fresh tomato may be added if desired.
Light Vegetable Soup
To 1½ cups of chicken stock add 1 cup of diced vegetables, e.g. pumpkin, sweet potato, carrot, leek, celery, in any combination, and a tablespoon of rolled oats or rice. Add ½ cup of water, simmer for 15-20 minutes.
Vegetable Cream Soup
Add puréed boiled pumpkin, carrot, sweet potato, broccoli, asparagus or spinach to chicken stock in equal ratio of stock to vegetables. Heat to boiling then simmer 2 minutes. Stir in a little cream and season to taste.

Create Your Own Sauce

After pan frying chicken, add ½ to ¾ cup chicken stock to the pan, stir over low heat and scrape up all the brown cooked-on juices. Add wine or fruit juice, herbs or spices, a dash of cream or a little flour thickening, simmer for a minute then pour over the cooked chicken. A crushed plain biscuit or gingernut biscuit makes a good thickener for sauces.

Handy Tips

Do not let your stock liquid boil continuously as it will turn cloudy. It is best to let it gently simmer.

White pepper is stronger than black pepper. It is ground from ripe pepper - use about half as much as black pepper.

Gravy and sauces may be thickened by adding 2 teaspoons of cornflour, blended with a little water, added slowly to the sauce or liquid.

Cooking is not an exact science: one does not require finely calibrated scales, pipettes and scientific equipment to cook, yet the conversion to metric measures in some countries and its interpretations must have intimidated many a good cook.

Weights are given in the recipes only for ingredients such as meats, fish, poultry and some vegetables. Though a few grams/ounces one way or another will not affect the success of your dish.

Though recipes have been tested using the Australian Standard 250ml cup, 20ml tablespoon and 5ml teaspoon, they will work just as well with the US and Canadian 8fl oz cup, or the UK 300ml cup. We have used graduated cup measures in preference to tablespoon measures so that proportions are always the same. Where tablespoon measures have been given, these are not crucial measures, so using the smaller tablespoon of the US or UK will not affect the recipe's success. At least we all agree on the teaspoon size.

For breads, cakes and pastries, the only area which might cause concern is where eggs are used, as proportions will then vary. If working with a 250ml or 300ml cup, use large eggs (60g/2oz), adding a little more liquid to the recipe for 300ml cup measures if it seems necessary. Use the medium-sized eggs (55g/1^1/$_4$oz) with 8fl oz cup measure. A graduated set of measuring cups and spoons is recommended, the cups in particular for measuring dry ingredients. Remember to level such ingredients to ensure their accuracy.

English measures
All measurements are similar to Australian with two exceptions: the English cup measures 300ml/ 10fl oz, whereas the Australian cup measure 250ml/8fl oz. The English tablespoon (the Australian dessertspoon) measures 14.8ml/^{1}/$_2$fl oz against the Australian tablespoon of 20ml/^{3}/$_4$fl oz.

American measures
The American reputed pint is 16fl oz, a quart is equal to 32fl oz and the American gallon, 128fl oz. The Imperial measurement is 20fl oz to the pint, 40fl oz a quart and 160fl oz one gallon.

The American tablespoon is equal to 14.8ml/ ^{1}/$_2$fl oz, the teaspoon is 5ml/^{1}/$_6$fl oz. The cup measure is 250ml/8fl oz, the same as Australia.

Dry measures
All the measures are level, so when you have filled a cup or spoon, level it off with the edge of a knife. The scale below is the "cook's equivalent"; it is not an exact conversion of metric to imperial measurement. To calculate the exact metric equivalent yourself, use 2.2046 lb = 1kg or 1 lb = 0.45359kg

Metric		Imperial		
g = grams		oz = ounces		
kg = kilograms		lb = pound		
15g		^{1}/$_2$oz		
20g		^{2}/$_3$oz		
30g		1oz		
60g		2oz		
90g		3oz		
125g		4oz	^{1}/$_4$ lb	
155g		5oz		
185g		6oz		
220g		7oz		
250g		8oz	^{1}/$_2$ lb	
280g		9oz		
315g		10oz		
345g		11oz		
375g		12oz	^{3}/$_4$ lb	
410g		13oz		
440g		14oz		
470g		15oz		
1,000g	1kg	35.2oz	2.2 lb	
	1.5kg		3.3 lb	

Oven temperatures
The Celsius temperatures given here are not exact; they have been rounded off and are given as a guide only. Follow the manufacturer's temperature guide, relating it to oven description given in the recipe. Remember gas ovens are hottest at the top, electric ovens at the bottom and convection-fan forced ovens are usually even throughout. We included Regulo numbers for gas cookers which may assist. To convert °C to °F multiply °C by 9 and divide by 5 then add 32.

Oven temperatures

	C°	F°	Regulo
Very slow	120	250	1
Slow	150	300	2
Moderately slow	150	325	3
Moderate	180	350	4
Moderately hot	190-200	370-400	5-6
Hot	210-220	410-440	6-7
Very hot	230	450	8
Super hot	250-290	475-500	9-10

Cake dish sizes

Metric	Imperial
15cm	6in
18cm	7in
20cm	8in
23cm	9in

Loaf dish sizes

Metric	Imperial
23x12cm	9x5in
25x8cm	10x3in
28x18cm	11x7in

Liquid measures

Metric	Imperial	Cup & Spoon
ml	fl oz	
millilitres	fluid ounce	
5ml	$^1/_6$fl oz	1 teaspoon
20ml	$^2/_3$fl oz	1 tablespoon
30ml	1fl oz	1 tablespoon plus 2 teaspoons
60ml	2fl oz	$^1/_4$ cup
85ml	$2^1/_2$fl oz	$^1/_3$ cup
100ml	3fl oz	$^3/_8$ cup
125ml	4fl oz	$^1/_2$ cup
150ml	5fl oz	$^1/_4$ pint, 1 gill
250ml	8fl oz	1 cup
300ml	10fl oz	$^1/_2$ pint
360ml	12fl oz	$1^1/_2$ cups
420ml	14fl oz	$1^3/_4$ cups
500ml	16fl oz	2 cups
600ml	20fl oz 1 pint,	$2^1/_2$ cups
1 litre	35fl oz 1 $^3/_4$ pints,	4 cups

Cup measurements

One cup is equal to the following weights.

	Metric	Imperial
Almonds, flaked	90g	3oz
Almonds, slivered, ground	125g	4oz
Almonds, kernel	155g	5oz
Apples, dried, chopped	125g	4oz
Apricots, dried, chopped	190g	6oz
Breadcrumbs, packet	125g	4oz
Breadcrumbs, soft	60g	2oz
Cheese, grated	125g	4oz
Choc bits	155g	5oz
Coconut, desiccated	90g	3oz
Cornflakes	30g	1oz
Currants	155g	5oz
Flour	125g	4oz
Fruit, dried (mixed, sultanas etc)	185g	6oz
Ginger, crystallised, glace	250g	8oz
Honey, treacle, golden syrup	315g	10oz
Mixed peel	220g	7oz
Nuts, chopped	125g	4oz
Prunes, chopped	220g	7oz
Rice, cooked	155g	5oz
Rice, uncooked	220g	7oz
Rolled oats	90g	3oz
Sesame seeds	125g	4oz
Shortening (butter, margarine)	250g	8oz
Sugar, brown	155g	5oz
Sugar, granulated or caster	250g	8oz
Sugar, sifted icing	155g	5oz
Wheatgerm	60g	2oz

Length

Some of us still have trouble converting imperial length to metric. In this scale, measures have been rounded off to the easiest-to-use and most acceptable figures.

To obtain the exact metric equivalent in converting inches to centimetres, multiply inches by 2.54 whereby 1 inch equals 25.4 millimetres and 1 millimetre equals 0.03937 inches.

Metric	Imperial
mm=millimetres	in = inches
cm=centimetres	ft = feet
5mm, 0.5cm	$^1/_4$in
10mm, 1.0cm	$^1/_2$in
20mm, 2.0cm	$^3/_4$in
2.5cm	1in
5cm	2in
8cm	3in
10cm	4in
12cm	5in
15cm	6in
18cm	7in
20cm	8in
23cm	9in
25cm	10in
28cm	11in
30cm	1 ft, 12in

index